Animals

Miles Salter is a writer, musician and storyteller based in York. His first novel for teenagers, *A Song For Nicky Moon*, was shortlisted for the Times/Chicken House children's writing award in 2010. He has written for several newspapers including *The Guardian* and *The Independent*. He is a visiting lecturer in Creative Writing at Leeds Trinity University, and is director of York Literature Festival.

Miles's poems have appeared in some of the UK's leading poetry magazines, including *The Rialto, Ambit, Orbis* and *South Bank Poetry*. His first collection of poetry (writing as Miles Cain), *The Border*, was published by Valley Press in 2011.

Animals

Miles Salter

VP

Valley Press

First published in 2013 by Valley Press
Woodend, The Crescent, Scarborough, YO11 2PW
www.valleypressuk.com

ISBN: 978-1-908853-28-8
Cat. no.: VP0048

A CIP record for this book is
available from the British Library

Printed and bound in Great Britain by
Imprint Digital, Upton Pyne, Exeter

www.valleypressuk.com/authors/milessalter

Contents

for Helen

Acknowledgements

Acknowledgements are due to the editors of the following publications or websites, in which some of these poems, or versions of them, first appeared: *Ambit, Antiphon, Beyond The Walls: New Writing From York St John University, Beautiful Scruffiness, Cake, Eclectic Eel, Indigo Rising, Morning Star, Morphog, Poetry and Persuasion, Rialto, Segora Competition Pamphlet 2012, Turbulence, Troubadour Prize 2012.*

'White Room' resulted from a writing residency at New School House gallery in York, December 2012.

The title of 'Ten Reasons Why This World Must End Soon' was a phrase on a placard held by a religious gentleman in the centre of York in Summer 2011.

Thanks are due to Oz Hardwick, Carole Bromley, Jo Shapcott, Daljit Nagra and Abi Curtis for editorial suggestions. In addition, thanks to Kate Fox, Andy Humphrey, Ian McMillan, Jamie McGarry, Helen Mort, Christopher North, Carolina Read, Anna Saunders and Robert Teed for their help in different ways.

The photograph on the cover is from a work by Edward Hart (1847 – 1928) and can be seen at Castle Ward, County Down, Northern Ireland. Picture used by courtesy of National Trust Collections.

'The only book that is worth writing is the one
we don't have the strength or courage to write.
The book that hurts us (we who are writing),
that makes us tremble, redden, bleed.'

Hélène Cixous, *Three Steps on the Ladder of Writing* (1993)

Two by Two

after Julian Barnes

There were scraps, of course – monkeys snapped at snakes,
dogs yelled at parrots, sheep went delirious with panic.

Pandemonium. And all the while, Noah's eyes bulged.
He waved his arms, spat, shouted at Japheth and Shem

as the rain made everything a quagmire, which was fine
for the ducks, water voles and otters, but the cats went mental.

One hamster was flattened by an elephant.
Two pandas, fresh into their tiny mating window

(a day and a half and she loses interest for another year)
seemed pre-occupied. Ants queued up at the flattened hamster.

'Two by two,' bellows Noah, as if suffering from some
obsession with order. It was hopeless. Birds flew

from the boat, beetles headed for soaking shrubbery,
ducks undulated away on the waves.

The last hippo, slick with brown mud, was heaved on board
by six humans, and the door was bolted shut.

In the darkness, a mess of claw and feather and noise.
As for me, I flew to the top of the boat with my sister,

watched the rain applaud itself, and spied, far off,
a whale squirting water into the air.

Their Eyes Were Not Watching God

because nobody had ever been to one of his parties
and said how amazing it was, and because the deity
never turned up on a TV show like *Britain's Got Talent*.
If he was so all-powerful, why didn't he train a dog,
or do some magic, or play some jazz-funk licks
on the saxophone? There were disputes
about God's age and gender, and whether
or not he was a psychopath. Critics cited lines
in the Old Testament about smiting enemies,
or his hatred of men having sex with other men,
even though the Almighty had produced some
pretty weird shit with animals. Worst of all
was God's intimidating silence, as if he
couldn't be bothered. The world, in return,
ignored him, although prayers were uttered
by the desperate, or Brazilian footballers during penalty
shoot outs at World Cup Finals. The faithful
turned up for mass or communion,
accepting wafers beneath slim alabaster men with
despairing eyes and blood that trickled down
pure white feet. But most people found this presentation
a little disturbing, and their eyes did not watch Mary
in her crisp blue shawl, and they didn't read
about superfluity of naughtiness, but turned instead
to *EastEnders* or *Coronation Street*,
where the language was plainer and there wasn't much need
for guilt or forgiveness, and one sin generally led
to another drum-roll, another episode, and eternity
was measured in brief voyeuristic kicks,
with several million viewers watching religiously.

Lot Remembers Sarah

Genesis 19:26

Heads gripped by emergency,
our feet scuffed the dust as the shadow
of the city loomed at our backs.
Run. Run. The breath ragged
in our throats, the ground red and dry,
survival trembling on the horizon.

Half a mile from the walls, I could not hear
the panic pulsing through her mouth
or her feet slipping on the sand.
That night, alone in the flapping tent,
I imagined clinging to her bleached body,
twisted towards the town, and saw myself
kissing her frozen mouth, my tongue
dislodging a crumb of salt.

Knock

Luke 11:9

I stand before the door, knuckles raised. Even
though I have been here many times (and the
door has always remained shut), I believe that
this time it will be different. I believe this time
things will change. This time, the door will be
opened. I have no idea what I am going to find
on the other side but I hope there will be sunlit
pastures, perhaps a Wurlitzer playing Sam
Cooke. A Change Is Gonna Come. There is no
way of knowing. Some urge within me says *go
on, knock, do it*, and I'm about to knock. My heart
is jumping in my chest sweat leaks through my
forehead. I breathe in and look at the door, which
is still closed. I hear a noise behind me and turn to
see a queue of people, waiting their turn to knock.
One of them shuffles, mumbles. Another coughs,
looks at a watch. I turn back to the door and

Turn It Down

'…and his heart like people who can
only tolerate a certain dose of music…'
– Gustave Flaubert, *Madame Bovary*

He never rushed to Woolworth's
for *Sergeant Pepper* or *Blonde on Blonde,*

didn't pause for choirs climaxing
at Hallelujah, or brass bands puffing

near Christmas. He did not take
his kids to churning stadiums

where thousands roared for encores;
ignored buskers rummaging through

The Four Seasons, avoided sniffing
at car boots for the torn face of Howling Wolf.

And when he died, the Vicar wanted
tales of work and family. 'And music?'

the Reverend asked. 'What could we play?
Mozart? Elvis? Something else?'

The deceased's daughter stared back,
a dozen chords locked inside her throat.

The Devil Invents Rock 'n' Roll

It was my greatest hit;
the beat for capitalism
and innuendo, a soundtrack
retching from the suburbs.

Some Southern kid flashed his hips
and girls clutched their cheeks.
Preachers rehearsed hysteria
for bouts of weekend pandemonium.

I crept inside verses.
Sympathy For the Devil,
A Highway to Hell. My eyes
shone from souvenir merchandise.

I snared tragedy in blues,
sex in 4/4 time. Old bandmates
crawled through hellish tours
to despise each other.

Groupies bent for cocaine,
pouted in dressing rooms
as lonely singers made carnage
of themselves.

Last summer, at the stadium,
I stood in backstage shadow.
As managers weighed cash
and the crowd called out for more,
I flipped a coin and struck a match.

Jimmy Savile Speaks

Now then, now then, howzabout the public?
They're glad that I run, raise money,
sign autographs. All is well, you see. What's
wrong with a cigar on the running machine?
Here's a picture of me with Elvis. I'm special,
baby, number one. I tramp around the country
like a grey timber wolf, a wild animal. I've got needs,
I've got a caravan, you see. The girls walk in
for food, perfume, a flash of words.
These eyes can hypnotise. I tell the driver
to get a cup of tea, then it's *Top of the Pops*,
gold records, hits. Fixed. Nobody seems to mind.
I like the hospitals, the way a face can open wards,
and there's always somebody you can be familiar with.
The thrills you get without love. I'm an OBE,
I'm on TV. I keep her majesty amused. Next.
Look at this face. It's all about me me me me me.

Ears

When the night is too vast,
too black, or the TV's slick cheer
makes him clutch his head,
he sits in the centre of the thin house
and holds the tin.

There's the one with the intact
hoop of gold, another from a grey lady
who never heard. The battered triangle
from a cat's head. He calls them his.

Lighting a candle, he takes one
from the box, holds it in his palm
and starts. 'It's like this,' he says.

Cat

I am eyes. I am ears. I am paws and teeth
and claws like thin moons. I have a tongue,

and whiskers that twitch when I twist
around doors, tail up, giving a small

grunt of welcome. I know high places
where I store the world inside my face.

In the day when the house is soft and quiet,
I find a bed and make a circle of myself.

Later, with eyes full of smell, ears full of dark,
I look for a mouse that will soon be tired.

The Dogs

They come at midnight,
sniffing, jumping, asking after you.

'No', I say, staring at the moon.
They have begun to look senile,
their muzzles turning grey, eyes
milky with lack of sight. 'Get down.'

They are aimless now, skittering
at pavements, jaws full of yawning.
I want to caress, say heel, walkies.
It's no use. I know they're lost

to the night, a longing for life,
the absence of gravitation a good training
might have brought. They won't sit up,
roll over, play dead for anyone.

I hear their snarls and yelps
recede in the dark, until all
that's left is a barking inside my eye.

Tex Avery's Wolf, 1943

Dressed in a tux, he whistles at the tease
in the spotlight, slams the table with his fists

and a chair, sets up a machine of whistles
and clapping hands, stares until his eyes

leap from his head. There is nothing
he can do to curb his instincts

as the unbelievable blonde in long white gloves
sings 'Oh Wolfy, ain't you the one?'

Bull

after Pablo Picasso, 'Minotaur Attacking An Amazon', 1933

At night the rampage begins, our herd
swarming through soft trees, ignoring
the branches that snap at our thighs
as we stamp across streams, shunt past
roots, flatten the thick grass beneath
our hooves.

We snuffle through darkness, blind
to anything except instinct and scent.
We forget the draconian wind, the moon,
our filthy, matted skin, and find our way
to the woman. Towering over her, one of us
is a solid cloud of muscle and horn.

Liar

Listen. Come close. A hundred new
and delicate promises gather
in my mouth; all the words
you want to hear, the soft pitch
and reel of my voice bringing reward,
gossip, all the suggestions
your petty heart can take.
Every phrase is a jewel, a potion,
a charm against indifference, so lean in,
honey, sugar, darling, babe.
My phrases will make your head nod
until you're besotted with surrender.
There will be no violence, coercion,
or arms turned against spines.
This is not witchcraft. These are only
consonants and vowels. Nothing more.

Confession

Suddenly, Father, I glared at the truth;
the hours we spent crouching in grass,
rushing at wildebeest, opening their throats,

staining our fur with warm flesh.
We blinked in the savannah,
never pondering the lives we finished

as we ambled away from the junk,
leaving a gift of ribcage for
frantic vultures and early flies.

There is nothing, my mother said,
except muscle and instinct, but I've dared
to stare at our habits and walk away.

I've informed my siblings, who laughed
and bit my head. It took a long time
to walk here and I want to hear you

say the words, *go in peace*, whatever. But wait.
Something itches in my paws,
a stubborn memory stays on my tongue.

I feel strange. I'm not used to curtains
and incense. Forgive me. Lay hands on me,
then lead me from wilderness and bone.

Giraffe

Giraffe walks into a bar and says
'Is this some kind of joke? I can't
even stand up straight. I feel tense.'

'Have a drink, love,' says the barman, winking
at George, one of the regulars. 'It might help.'
He turns, fills a small glass with Glenfiddich.

A bubble rises in the bottle.
The giraffe tries to drink
but the glass yells against the floor.

The animal stares, kicks a stool.
'I need to get out,' she says, treading
on glass, blood seeping from her hoof.

'This is all wrong. I should be in Africa.
I want the grassland, the wind, the taste of acacia
in the slope of my neck. Not the coarse talk of saloons.

You call this freedom? Cinzano and pork scratchings?
What are you, animals?' The barman sighs,
turns back to George, who stifles a belch,

pushes four coins across the bar.
The Giraffe bangs her head
against the fruit machine,
eyes rolling like cherries.

The Only Thing I Had Left To Sell Was My Soul

The credit card shone in my palm as I hit
the high street, hopped to *Next, Gap, Fat Face*,
came home weighted with bags, looked
the business, was hot stuff. Got a car, a house,
a week with sun cream and bloody cocktails,
ate meals in cool rooms with high ceilings,
bought ceramic swans and vast coffee table tomes.
Hardly thought about APR or small print.
Things stayed placid until the letters turned red
and the summons came. I stared at the row of zeros,
swallowed, sweated, started to sell what I had.
The clothes went to car boots in fresh autumn mornings.
I sold my pets, time, body, felt numb, stuffed
fading gold into envelopes. I rented my forehead
as advertising space, flogged a kidney for a grand
and lay in Ward 17, depleted, washed out, haggard,
finished. The only thing I had left to sell was my soul.
As a man in a suit leaned over my hospital bed,
I wept for the dinners and Spanish sunsets.
'You're six quid short,' he said, offering me a pen
or a scalpel, it was hard to tell through the tears.
'Sign here, and I'm gone.' He almost smiled.
Outside, priceless birds were dancing in the breeze.

World Without End

Honest, we had no inkling. It was all normal,
going out and getting stuff, taking it home,
calling it ours. It was all we thought about,
some nights, the wages and what we could
get with them. The colours poured from screens

pushing kitchens, cars, chocolate.
Sex and smiles and nought
per cent finance. At weekends
we bought that quiet, single-minded
mania every time, looting shops

with plastic or cash, cramming cars with food,
toys, trinkets for pets, tiles, designer clothes,
disposable nappies, razors, cameras, barbecue sets.
Women in high heels pushed trolleys.
We didn't know better. I never thought about it

until I was forty six, when Hull
flooded and Bill from the factory was dragged
from the river, bloated and cold.
Janice was livid when she couldn't
get to Asda for pizza and tissues.

Course, it's different now. This generation
know another cost. Rationing and censorship.
You can't watch films from the old days, Brad Pitt
and James Bond are banned. All those cars, drinks,
people consuming. It's obscene, they say,

but we never thought it was odd. It was
how things went. I can't explain. I'm 73 now.
They kept me alive because I'm an electrician.
The highlands are popular, a dry space,
but a lot of flies, so I hear.

The Ledge

The sun was blinding at the ledge,
turning us thirsty, delirious. We peered
at the drop, whistled at gravity
as Joe kicked a pebble into air
and watched it turn to nothing.
We were exhausted, dirty,
our clothes turned to strips of grey cloth
on the journey of bleached dawns
past prehistoric cars, junked prams
and bones. The old world done.

We sat all day, talking about how times
used to be, the stuff we could buy.
Cars. Shampoo. Lager and thrills.
We shared our final tin of corned beef,
then lay down, head to head.
My arm rested beside the drop
into darkness. Wind scarred our ears
as I called Joe's name, told him I loved him.

In the morning a vulture flapped
four feet from my nose.
I batted it away with my arm,
called Joe's name. He was gone;
must have turned over in his sleep,
or else struck out on his own.
Drops of rain patted my cheek and nose
as the vulture flapped into the air, eyed me up,
then caught a breeze and fell from view.

A Warning

They limp from the marshes, trenches,
beaches and streams, spitting salt water,
blood, bits of plastic, complaining of tides

and blisters. They carry burnt flags. Their
mouths are smudged with dirt and sweat;
pockets crammed with bags holding crumbs.

Some are blind, some bald, and some stare
like lizards. Others hobble and stagger.
Welts and bruises cover their groins.

They circle our immaculate village, start
shouting our names and something about the future.
We retreat to watch dancers on a screen and pull

corks from bottles. The strangers stay
for two weeks, day and night muttering
at our hedges and extensions.

Phil at number 12 talks about legal action,
calls the Police. The officers park cars and mobilise
bollards, speak to the visitors in low voices.

A dog is kicked, a greenhouse gets cracked,
somebody lobs a Coke can and a mobile phone. The next
morning they are gone, leaving circles in the mud.

We shrug and nod at each other, climb into cars,
stare at screens. Later, we realise those
limping creatures resembled our kids.

The Queue

'Jesus, the heat,' says Karen. She's not wrong. Eighteen hours we've been queuing and moved forward two feet. It's like the whole planet has turned up in one place where there are no cash machines, mobile phone signals or coffee outlets. The sun is demonic, and tall men holding whips take our watches, rings, small change. We are barefoot. Sand blows around our nostrils. Several people have passed out, including the man from Surrey who dealt in futures. We do not know how long the wait will be. 'Is there a hold up?' I ask one of the men. He smiles but says nothing. He has large muscles and good teeth, seems relaxed. But up ahead, some bloke is raging, head red as a lobster, sick with too much sun, and he's kicking off real bad, shouting Achtung something. Karen says he was asking for protein, but was taken away in a van that patrols the queue. Karen says she'll see what the hold up is. I give her my water bottle and hat, then watch as she walks out of sight. That night the temperature crashes. I lie with other humans to keep warm. A woman from Romford wants to kiss me. Her mouth smells of red wine. 'Not much of a life is it?' she asks. It's days before Karen comes back, face red, looking older. She shakes her head, says 'the things I've seen.' 'What?' I ask. 'Are there toilets? Mattresses?' She tells me about the front of the queue, the city walls, the guards, the tiny, inadequate doorway, the mewling crowds of humans jostling for entry, malnourished, diseased, blown up, ripped off. 'Those kids up there,' Karen mutters, pointing to the front of the queue. 'Nothing but skin and eyes. We'll have to wait our turn.'

Apology

for Ruby

The night I cracked
your bare behind
with my palm

(three times bigger,
eighteen times older
than yours), I lost something.

Your mouth gaped
in alarm, then looped
a cry for your mother.

The bath water you stood in became
a trickle, a stream, a river
that carried you away from me.

Spiders

At the end of the bridge, staking their claim
to a blinding bulb at the edge of Autumn,
I lost count of tiny spiders in overlapping webs,
waiting for flies to fall for the glamour of light.

Evening

He pauses at the children's doors,
listens for the air slipping
backwards and forwards in their lungs.
It comforts him. Downstairs, they talk.
She tells him if he needs deodorant, says
she is bothered about the ironing.
The washing up leans beneath drips.
At night, sometimes, he can't sleep
for fear of what may come into the world,
a terrible cloud, a vast and vicious raven,
spreading across the globe, shouting his name
so loud it defeats his own heartbeat.
'This world bothers me,' he tells her. 'The kids.'
'Sweetheart,' she says.
They hold each other before sleep.

The Gift

The stranger arrived in late afternoon,
wiped his shining face with a spotted rag.
Three medals flapped at his chest. We sat
on the doorstep, Carrie and me, ice creams
bitten to ragged cones, a day so hot
the rooftops wobbled.

It was the middle of June. We'd spent
a week sprinting through parks, prancing
near sprinklers, aiming water pistols
at cats hiding in flowerbeds. We knew
nothing but laughter and the price of liquorice.

The stranger held a tiny case, said
it was a gift. 'Remember what Mum said,'
Carrie hissed. The man clicked the clasps
and opened the lid. Night spilled
from the small walls of the box.

A black line spread across lawns and roses,
brought a sudden, sunless chill. Carrie ran
for a coat as rain fell to clicking roofs, turned to sleet,
turned to snow. There was nowhere to go.
We shouted, flung balls from pink hands,

then stumbled home to bed as, streets away,
sirens made a mess of the quiet. From the window
we peered at the man on the pavement,
his bowed and penitent head, his folded hands.
In the morning, we rummaged at curtains
to find a blue and faultless sky.

The man was gone, the small case remained,
upside down in the road. 'What shall
we do now?' Carrie asked. We buried the box
at the back of the Church, but three nights later,
I lay awake in bed, biting the pillow as Carrie
slept in the room next door.

Exposure

They have taken my clothes and strapped me
to the front of the car. A tall woman
wearing leather boots looks down, smiles.
I ask her for a mask. She says nothing.
Despite the cold, sweat leaks through
my forehead. My hands are pulled behind me,
tied to black handles at the side of the car.
The woman produces lipstick, writes
my name on the bonnet, then drives
away from the farm. She turns on the radio.
Light jazz vibrates at the wrong speed.
The car arrives at the centre of town
where everybody I ever kissed or shook hands with
stares at my knees, navel and throat.
My mother and father know what I have
been accused of. Dogs bark, crows wait
on chimneys. A man with a rope stands
by a wooden pillar. This will not last, I tell myself.
Above, the moon is silent. 'In The Mood'
comes to an end. Beyond the church, men with torches
are streaming down from the hills.

Learning to Crawl

I smashed my head on life itself: affairs
and overtime turned me blue and black,
bureaucracy did my head in, addictions
left me gasping for a wholeness I could
not name. I railed and swore at bosses
and lovers who all turned away, shaking
their heads. I drove my car into a wall. An
ambulance took what was left of me, fed
me anaesthetic, placed me in bandages
and intensive care. An old man arrived
and held my hand. He said nothing but
stayed for weeks. The doctors said I
would not walk again. But the presence,
beside me, one hand on mine, made me
strong. Now, the nurses put the old man
at one of end of the corridor, and me at
the other. I crawl towards him, craving
the kindness in his mouth and eye. It will
take me years to reach him, and by the
time I arrive, he'll be gone. By then, I'll
know enough to sit next to some young
sod, lying smashed up and ready to be
healed.

A Burial

In the email, I told her
I'd felt like an animal, or a child.

I hated the way she saw me shrivel,
curling into memory and anguish.

I drove away, knowing
I'd never fix myself.

Hack

News International, Summer 2011

Show me the desk, the P.A., the expense account,
the money, the contract, the palms of lawyers.
Show me the invitations to private functions,
the menu, the opportunities. Let me hear the gossip
becoming column inches, the conversations
of the celebrity injured, the clicks in the machine,
the fresh angle, the circulation figures.
Show me the story, the money, the glass doors
Swinging open, the cheek of the Prime Minister,
the clothes of his wife, the actual words the footballer used,
the money, the column inches, the industrial shredder.
Show me the pale eyes of the billionaire, the way
he enters a room, the cash inside his cough.
Show me the faces of the staff as I tell them it's over.
But not for me, my nerve, my fist.
The headlines stay safe in my brain.

Hollywood Without Animals

No Lassie. No Bambi. No Garfield. No Paws.
No Black Beauty. No Birds. No Gremlins. No Jaws.

Your Country Needs You

to leave your children, wives and kitchens
and learn how to fire and reload; to go to France
and dig into the ground; to follow orders; to sing
songs in the rain about Tipperary. Your Country
Needs You to live in a landscape without trees,
to dwell with rats in water, to share rations
from a metal box, to write cheerful letters
home, to walk across a field in daylight as
bullets plough through ribcages, kidneys
and brains. Your Country Needs You to plunge
a bayonet into the enemy, to smash the butt
of your gun into his face, creasing his teeth
and nose until he falls backwards with a shrug.
Your Country Needs You to forget the rules
of cricket and become a man who sweats
and screams in his sleep, a man who beats
his wife and daughter, a man who saw
the stern eyes, dark moustache, pointing figure
and did what he was told.

Gun

She anchors herself in routine;
drink, meal, bath, screen.
In the bedroom she hears her feet,
feels the cool metal beneath the pillow.

What happened was a trigger.
She swore a second time
a man would end up ruined
by a finger's twitch,

then slips to illusion.
Bullets doze in a clip,
point at red flowers
clambering up the wall.

In the morning her dreams flee
as the city starts to growl.
She unhooks the door three times,
then places herself in the chamber of the day.

Drone Talking

You do not understand how good it is
to work without guilt, or tears.
But then, neither do I, never knowing
cold, or anxiety, or the mad incentive
to push your child to the ground
as an incendiary drops from the sky.

And some might say it is better to live
this way, moving steadily through
cool air without panic or hesitation,
approaching the target, completing
the task with thoroughness
and precision, then turning
above smoke and flame, knowing
there is no possibility of error.

White Room

for John Lennon, December 2012

The shops bleat Christmas as grinning snowmen
disguise a tidal lust for cash. This room drifts
into winter: white walls, white chairs,
white umbrellas pointing to art. I could fetch
a clicking copy of *The White Album* and stick
it on the turntable, imagine you with a guitar
in the porch at Aunt Mimi's house, before flashes
of screaming cheeks, then your white room,
a white piano, imagine all the people. Ten years
later and Strawberry Fields and Mr Kite
become graffiti on a New York sidewalk.
Three decades later and the slaughtered dead
are white with rage. They hiss from their graves
in Gaza, Bazra, Homs, New York. They say
'Keep singing, John. We need you to tell them:
Give peace a chance.'

The Big Society

The trick is in the phrasing. Use first names,
say 'I don't accept that.' Leave the studio
when the ON AIR light turns dull. Walk to the car,
wait for a text from the boys at Number 10.

A row of meetings. What will happen if.
Stick to it. Look strong. Meet the others
in the bar, a table at The Ivy, good burgundy,
Lawrence's cousin. Share options,

a place on the board. Then home, avoiding
streets where the houses of the unseen
hold blue screens shining with soaps.
They weren't at Eton, they can't talk,

think, write the same; the cleaners, bus drivers,
builders, the ones from stacked streets, walking
dogs near graffiti, the ones we keep away from.
Another interview. Remember the phrases;

the Big Society. We're all in this together.
Dinner tomorrow. Lawrence's cousin, venison,
laughter. Percentages and foie gras,
while the country shrinks in the dark.

Disrupted

London riots, August 2011

Imagine glass repairing itself,
deleting injuries from bricks or boots,
packets of fags still on shelves,
vodka and trainers untouched.

Imagine a place in middle England,
the church bells ringing, ducks
on a pond, taxes paid, a phone call
from Mum, gravy and a tidy bed.

Imagine a television, not ripped
from the high street by a manic,
running herd, its screen never showing
your half-covered face, but bought

with honest cash, grown from
timesheets and weeks at work,
carried away without reprisal,
fire or panic. Imagine that.

Longhill

for Sharon Childs

Remember the nights, Sharon, when we plagued
those streets, hunting chances for compassion.
Standing outside the tiny, suffocating shops,
we watched a mass of lads spin a ball

between intoxication and theft.
In buzzing summer air younger ones
ran from houses, shouting our names
over concrete and grass. Parents checked distances.

We did our best: school assemblies
and baking clubs, line dancing in a leaking hall,
talent shows, community, good practice,
endurance. We reported on graffiti,

charred cars, youths swinging from probation
to C Wing. I stored misfortunes
from the roads. The boy who tried to rob us.
The night my car was taken.

We traded in rumours. A pregnancy. Police.
Wounds the size of houses. You gave precautions
to the girls with vast earrings and expensive faces
as my trainers squeaked in streets laced with rain.

A fresh and sober knowledge dribbled on my eyelids.
A line of weighted shadows. The way things dwindle.
The windy October night, two years after starting,
when we filed our report, swung the door shut, and looked
   for home.

Futures

A day is coming, you tell the mirror,
when your arms will swing beneath
blossom by the clean and steady river,
knowing every conversation deposits

insight. The slow and quick will offer
palms and invitations to coffee,
while traffic wardens issue jokes
instead of fines. Lean, smiling children

will run in the park without boredom
or phones, shadows won't lean across
the shoulders of mothers. Strangers will
open car doors in the rain, say 'Hop in,'

without causing alarm. And on that day,
hedgerows won't harbour fading beer cans,
bicycles shall be admired but left alone,
pigeons and foxes trot across the road,

no problem, and those who choose
to discuss the weather will enjoy the process.
At night, double bass and trumpet
will spread warm, friendly anthems

through avenues at a party open to all.
Wine and bread will be passed around
by ex-looters. Hangovers will not trespass.

Gleaming cars will transport food
and clothing through checkpoints.
The market for surveillance cameras
shall collapse amid laughter.

Chaplains won't squeak through ticking wards,
while distant explosions transform into vast
and scented flowers. A day is coming, you tell
yourself. The clock ticks without prejudice.

Might

And then, one day, as the city ticked and lorries
proclaimed 'this vehicle is reversing,' a man glanced
up from accounts and saw them, all six of them,
ascend into the happy blue air, their little tails curling,
snorts of delight making tiny songs, just audible
through the hiss and rub of traffic. He watched
them grow smaller than commas, disappearing
to the west, then went to the stationary cupboard
to calm down. When a girl ate a bacon buttie at lunch,
the man wept openly in the canteen.

The Horse Rider's Code of Conduct

I understand that riding at any standard has inherent risk
and that all horses may react unpredictably on occasions.
I may fall off and could be injured. I accept that risk.
I understand that instructions are given for my safety and agree
to follow instructions given to me by staff and instructors
of the riding school. I reserve the right not to ride a horse
allocated to me but usually I am glad to get close to them,
to know their quietness, their present weight, their potent,
wise eyes and the way they stamp and toss their heads.
I love the way they crunch an apple, or the way they wait
when the farrier fits the shoe. I understand
that wearing an appropriate riding hat and body protector
may reduce the severity of an injury should an accident happen
and I agree that I will always wear a riding hat whilst riding,
leading and grooming horses at the riding school. I understand
it is my choice whether or not I wear a body protector
and I remember that morning last summer.
The stables were quiet. He was fresh from the night
and the sky was clear and the paths through the oaks and birches
were cool and empty. We kept going for an hour and the whole
world seemed to flood through me and I yelled out in a language
I didn't understand, and did not want to go back.

The Python Who Slept With A Woman

for Carolina Read

When a man got close, she reared up,
hissing, the whiff of his pheromones
sending her crazy. She climbed doorframes
until weight and gravity pulled her to the ground,
sought heat at the back of the television,
made documentaries topple over.

Remember the way she curled around you,
air pulsing from her nostrils, and the coils
of dense muscle on the bed at night –
the kind of weight against your thigh
that only comes from twenty feet of snake.

This Is Not You

This is not you – nodding at a girl in the cheap
part of the city, slipping her folded twenties for fifteen
messy minutes, back of a car, side road, radio on,
forgetting everything but the sound of her mouth.

This is not you. Screaming names at the salty
wind, over and over, 2am in darkness, feet
from the edge of the cliff, a mouth full of vodka,
saying fuck it, I'm done. They'll manage.

This is not you. Holding a gun and firing at men
in another country, sending hot metal into the eye of
somebody's brother. The adrenalin of kicks and fears
replaced by sofas and stale television.

This is you. Bathtimes with your child,
emails, phone calls. Petrol in the car,
bland conflicts repeated on screen,
cups of tea and fretting at weeds.
You're sober. You're clean. You're here.

School

Settle down please. The student manual
outlines the modules, we expect appearances
at lectures to be of a high standard. You may wear ties.
The course begins with manipulation for beginners,
followed by body language, oratory skill
and how to work a room. Firearms training
is optional. In our experience, there's a great deal
you can achieve by voice alone.

In the second semester, you'll learn
how to build a power base, develop
extortion techniques and utilise
latent prejudice to extend your influence.
Your practical exam will test your abilities
in thuggery. What you do with the body
will count towards your final marks.

By the end of the third year, you'll
be an expert in callousness, rigging
voting systems, abrupt and clandestine
violence. You'll know how to control
a population, deal with backhanders,
and employ a working knowledge
of basements, jump leads and ropes.

We find that student teamwork
diminishes near the end. There is hunger
in the corridors, whispers and fists.
The final exam requires no writing,
but, happily, a single baseball bat
will be available to the group.
We wish you well on your journey.
If there is any way we can help, please ask.
Good luck. We will see one of you at the end.

Photographs

And when it was done,
she sent back all the pictures
of the two of us together.

I opened a brown envelope
and out tumbled the weekend
in the Lakes when we'd walked

through dripping trees, her voice
calling me honey, a hundred
moments of her kindness.

It couldn't be helped. I sat, dumb
with grief, on the floor of my kitchen
and wept for what was done, felt

a mouth open inside me,
felt the sick pollution of fear
at another chance to be alone.

When I heard she was married
I sent a card, said I was sorry
if I'd hurt her, and how I was glad.

The Minutes

In the morning fresh minutes are waiting.
Hundreds crowd your bed, litter the floor.
There are so many, threading

down the stairs and out the door.
In the evening, as the sky darkens,
you look for the minutes but most

have gone. As you watch, another
vanishes. The phone rings.
Two minutes go.

In bed, you close your eyes
and ask for more.

Precision

for Carole Bromley

Some days I think of you, a pebble's leap
from our garden, fixing those nouns

and line breaks. Your pot of sharpened
pencils points to the ceiling, the sky,

the words in the stars,
and the stars in the words.

The Back of the Withdrawal Room

A room of dust and time; old green brickwork
and things gone. Eight brown box files marked
'London A Level'. Assorted screws. A barbecue
set. The wing of a bird, dropping dry feathers from
its supreme scaffold of bone. Two busted crabs
in a grimy flora tub. The skull of a dog. A baby
pig, quite white, upside down in a jar, back
flattened against the side. Its eyes shut, and
six legs provide an example of itself.

Ten Reasons Why This World Must End Soon

1) There are not enough elastic bands to go around. Soon India, China, and several South American countries will all be ordering Iron Maiden CDs and crime novels from Amazon. Postal workers will not be able to cope with the weight of cardboard and junk mail.

2) Humans find it hard to share.

3) There are more of us people arriving each day. Babies will grow up to own phones and carry coffee cups. We need more loyalty cards and bacon.

4) Jesus is returning, according to some. There may or may not be a Rapture, followed by Satan being at large. It's hard to tell how things will go. Either way, it's best not to do anything too risky. Stay at home. Eat ice cream. Have you tried Ben and Jerry's?

5) The ice caps only have so much time left. Try not to panic.

6) If they use the full arsenal at their disposal a lot of us will die quickly and others will die slowly. Look at the countries, the rhetoric. Iran. Israel. North Korea. Pakistan. USA. Syria. Russia. There will be rats.

7) Relax. All shall be well and all shall be well and all manner of thing shall be well. Watch *Friends*. Go to Starbucks. Give to charity. Shit happens.

8) Nothing lasts forever. 'Soon' may be a relative term. The sun will surrender, five billion years from now. You will not see this.

9) Imagine it. No rock and roll. No stock market.

10) The dust. The light. The silence defeating stars.